D1523422

MYERS-BRIGGS

Virginia Loh-Hagan

Published in the United States of America by Cherry Lake Publishing Group
Ann Arbor, Michigan
www.cherrylakepublishing.com

Reading Adviser: Marla Conn, MS, Ed., Literacy specialist, Read-Ability, Inc.
Book Designer: Felicia Macheske

Photo Credits: © Asier Romero/Shutterstock.com, cover; © STILLFX/Shutterstock.com, cover;
© Rido/Shutterstock.com, 5; © Syda Productions/Shutterstock.com, 6; © Daniel Jedzura/
Shutterstock.com, 9; © Dmytro Zinkevych/Shutterstock.com, 11; © YAKOBCHUK VIACHESLAV/
Shutterstock.com, 12; © pixelheadphoto digitalskillet/Shutterstock.com, 15; © sirtravelalot/
Shutterstock.com, 17; © Asier Romero/Shutterstock.com, 18; © Igor Tichonow/Shutterstock.com, 20;
© Monkey Business Images/Shutterstock.com, 22; © Lia Koltyrina/Shutterstock.com, 25; © HBRH/
Shutterstock.com, 27; © SpeedKingz/Shutterstock.com, 29

Graphics Throughout: © AKaiser/Shutterstock.com; © galastudio/Shutterstock.com;
© tanyabosyk/Shutterstock.com; © ViSnezh/Shutterstock.com; © MARINA ARABADZHI/
Shutterstock.com; © Alisa Burkovska/Shutterstock.com
Copyright © 2021 by Cherry Lake Publishing Group

45th Parallel Press is an imprint of Cherry Lake Publishing Group.

Library of Congress Cataloging-in-Publication Data

Names: Loh-Hagan, Virginia, author.
Title: Myers-Briggs / by Virginia Loh-Hagan.
Description: Ann Arbor, Michigan : Cherry Lake Publishing, [2020]
| Series: Who are you? | Includes index.
Identifiers: LCCN 2020006992 (print) | LCCN 2020006993 (ebook)
| ISBN 9781534169159 (hardcover) | ISBN 9781534170834 (paperback)
| ISBN 9781534172678 (pdf) | ISBN 9781534174511 (ebook)
Subjects: LCSH: Myers-Briggs Type Indicator—Juvenile literature.
       |
   Personality tests—Juvenile literature.
Classification: LCC BF698.8.M94 L64 2020 (print) | LCC BF698.8.M94
   (ebook) | DDC 155.2/83—dc23
LC record available at https://lccn.loc.gov/2020006992
LC ebook record available at https://lccn.loc.gov/2020006993

Cherry Lake Publishing Group would like to acknowledge the work of the Partnership for 21st
Century Learning, a Network of Battelle for Kids. Please visit *http://www.battelleforkids.org/
networks/p21* for more information.

Printed in the United States of America
Corporate Graphics

Dr. Virginia Loh-Hagan is an author, university professor, and former classroom teacher. She
took a free online Myers-Briggs personality test (www.truity.com). Her top three codes are ENFJ
(Teacher), ENTJ (Commander), and ESTJ (Director). She lives in San Diego, California, with her
very tall husband and very naughty dogs. To learn more about her, visit www.virginialoh.com.

Chapter One

A Special Test

What is the Myers-Briggs personality test like? What are some issues with it?

Myers-Briggs is a personality test. It's very popular. It's used all over the world. It's also called the Myers-Briggs Type **Indicator** (MBTI). Indicators are tools that reveal something. Myers-Briggs reveals people's personalities. It reveals their strengths and weaknesses. The test reveals people's likes and dislikes. It reveals possible jobs. The test even helps people determine who they're most **compatible** with. Compatible means getting along with others.

Myers-Briggs has many goals. First, it helps people understand themselves. Second, it helps people work better with others. Third, it helps people choose a future path. Fourth, it helps people learn better.

The MBTI is often used to help improve teamwork.
How would you describe yourself as a team player?

Myers-Briggs is a special test. It's an **inventory**. An inventory is like a checklist with many questions. Myers-Briggs has 93 questions. Each question has 2 choices.

People answer the questions. They **self-report**. This means they answer the questions based on what they think is true. There aren't right or wrong answers. There aren't any **norms**. Norms are standards. They're used to compare results against a "normal" or typical response. Myers-Briggs doesn't compare people to others. It just gives information about people's unique personalities.

Based on their answers, people are identified as a type. There are 16 different personality types. No one personality type is better than another. All types are equal. Every type has value.

There are many online tests. These are informal. The real MBTI is given by a trained person. Do you want to take the MBTI?

FUN FACTS

* Myers-Briggs has been translated into over 30 languages. It's used around the world.

* About 1.5 million people take the test online each year. Over 88 percent of Fortune 100 companies use it. They use it to hire and train.

* INFJ is the rarest Myers-Briggs type. Only about 1 percent of people score INFJ. Dr. Martin Luther King Jr. was an INFJ. These people care deeply about others. They want to ease suffering.

* The most common Myers-Briggs types are ISFJ, ESFJ, and ISTJ.

There are many studies on the Myers-Briggs test. Experts have said the test is **valid** and **reliable**. Valid means it measures what it says it does. Reliable means it produces the same results when given more than once.

Some experts disagree. They say the Myers-Briggs has "low test reliability." There were studies done. When people took the Meyers-Briggs test more than once over the span of a few weeks, the test produced different results. Some experts called Myers-Briggs an "**elaborate** Chinese fortune cookie." Elaborate means complicated or hard.

But people still use it. Myers-Briggs encourages people to reflect. It pushes people to think. People think about the scores. Then they compare the results to what they think about themselves. It's a starting point for change.

Some people don't like how there are only two choices per question. They don't think people fit into categories. What do you think?

Chapter Two

A Dynamic Duo

Who is Isabel Myers? Who is Katherine Briggs? Who is Carl Jung? How did the test develop?

Isabel Myers and Katherine Cook Briggs created the Myers-Briggs inventory. Briggs is Myers's mother.

Briggs lived from 1875 to 1968. She went to college at age 14. She graduated at the top of her class. When Isabel Myers was born, Briggs wanted to learn the best way to raise her. So, she studied **psychology**. Psychology is the study of human behavior. Briggs taught Myers at home. She homeschooled Myers. Briggs kept a journal. She called her living room a lab of "baby training." She wrote articles about child psychology.

Myers lived from 1897 to 1980. She met her husband, "Chief," at college. Briggs thought he was interesting. His personality was different.

Myers and Briggs are a mother-daughter team. Some people think the MBTI is criticized unfairly. They think it's because the creators are women. What do you think about that?

Chief inspired Briggs. Briggs went to the library. She studied the psychology of personalities.

Myers worked at an office. She hated it. Then she became a homemaker. She hated it. She wanted to find the perfect job. She thought jobs should match people's personalities.

Myers and Briggs found a common interest. They studied personalities. They taught themselves about the science of testing.

They created a personality test. They said it would help people find job matches. They did this around 1944.

Myers and Briggs were self-taught.
What have you taught yourself to do?

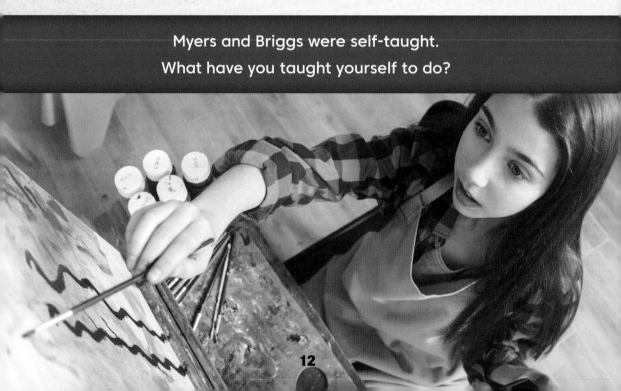

SCIENCE

Each personality type uses the brain in a different way. Brains have different areas. Each personality type uses one area more than other areas. This use of the brain is called brain activity. Dopamine is a chemical. It's in the brain. It helps humans think and feel. Everyone has the same amount of dopamine. But introverts are negatively affected by it. Introvert means shy and quiet. Extroverts are positively affected by dopamine. Extrovert means outgoing. Extroverts need more stimulation. Having the TV on could be noisy for introverts. It could be normal for extroverts. Dr. Dario Nardi studies brain science. He wrote a book called *Neuroscience of Personality: Brain Savvy Insights for All Types of People*. He studied brain activity of Myers-Briggs types. For example, ISTJ types show high activity in the back of their brains. This area deals with interpreting images. This is why ISTJ types tend to be visual learners.

The test became a hit. Myers and Briggs worked on it for the next 20 years. They kept improving it. They made it better.

Myers and Briggs based their work on Carl Jung's ideas. Jung lived from 1875 to 1961. He was from Switzerland. He was a **psychiatrist**. Psychiatrists are medical doctors who study the mind. Jung studied personalities. He believed there were 4 main types of personalities. He also developed the concept of extroverted and introverted personalities.

Briggs admired Jung. She called his work the "Bible." She even wrote him fan mail.

Jung was Briggs's role model. Do you have any role models? Who do you admire? Why?

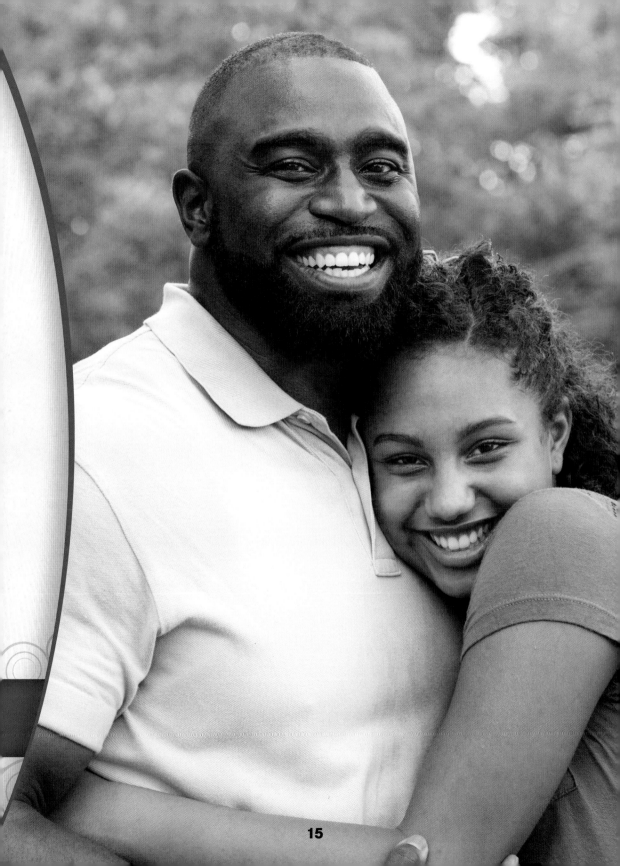

Chapter Three

MBTI Codes

What are the 16 personality types?

The inventory is sorted into 4 categories. People indicate their preferences in each category.

The first category focuses on how people get their energy.
- Extroversion (E) – This is a preference for action. Energy is gained from spending time with others.
- Introversion (I) – This is a preference for thinking, not acting. Energy is gained from being alone.

The second category focuses on how people deal with information.
- Sensing (S) – This is a preference for facts and details. Information is gained from using one's senses and experiences.
- Intuition (N) – This is a preference for interpreting or adding meaning. Information is gained from thinking about what's possible.

People have all these qualities. But we prefer certain qualities more than others. What are your preferences for each category?

The third category focuses on how people make decisions.

- **Thinking (T)** – This is a preference for facts and logic.
- **Feeling (F)** – This is a preference for **emotions**. Emotions are feelings.

The fourth category focuses on how people manage life.

- **Judging (J)** – This is a preference for making plans.
- **Perceiving (P)** – This is a preference for being flexible.

After completing the inventory, people get a Myers-Briggs code. This code has 4 letters. Each letter represents a category. The first letter is E or I. The second letter is S or N. The third letter is T or F. The fourth letter is J or P. There are 16 total personality types.

Think about some decisions you've made. What was the decision? How did you make the decision?

There are 8 types that are considered **observant**. Observant means paying attention to details.

These observant types are guardians. They're caring.
- ESFJ – This type is a provider. They give to others.
- ISFJ – This type is a protector. They care for others.
- ESTJ – This type is a director. They supervise.
- ISTJ – This type is an inspector. They check things.

These observant types are artists. They're hands-on.
- ESFP – This type is a performer. They demonstrate.
- ISFP – This type is a composer. They create.
- ESTP – This type is a promoter. They persuade others.
- ISTP – This type is a crafter. They make things.

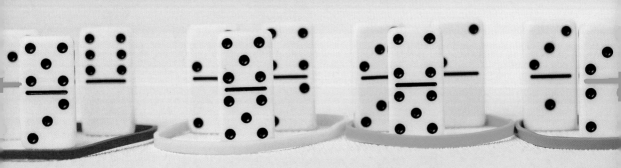

David Keirsey is a psychologist. He sorted the MBTI types into temperaments. What are other ways to sort the types?

Some authors are using Myers-Briggs to help them write. Claire Handscombe is ENFP. She's a British writer. She moved to Washington, D.C., in 2012. She writes fantasy and young adult books. Her first book is titled *Unscripted*. She uses Myers-Briggs to help develop her characters. As such, she's able to create characters outside of her own experiences. She said, "I was really stressed when I started because I didn't know what Myers-Briggs [type] my character was." She took an online Myers-Briggs test from the point of view of her character. She took other personality tests as well. This helped her get a better understanding of all her characters. Many writing coaches recommend using Myers-Briggs. Kristen Kieffer is an INFJ. She created an online writing resources community called "Well-Storied." She said, "Taking the Myers-Briggs test for any secondary characters receiving ample screen time helps ensure that they, too, feel as real as the people around me."

There are 8 types that are considered **introspective**. Introspective means reflective. These types are self-aware.

These introspective types are **idealists**. Idealists have noble goals. They have big dreams.
- INFJ – This type is an **advocate**. Advocates fight for their beliefs. They counsel others. They give guidance.
- ENFJ – This type is a teacher. They're givers.
- INFP – This type is a healer. They make peace.
- ENFP – This type is a champion. They motivate.

These introspective types are **rationalists**. Rationalists are thinkers. They're planners.
- INTJ – This type is a mastermind. They arrange things.
- ENTJ – This type is a commander. They prepare and organize people toward a goal.
- INTP – This type is a thinker. They design.
- ENTP – This type is an inventor. They come up with new ideas.

Think about these personality types.
Which types would you want on your team?

Chapter Four

FAMOUS EXAMPLES

Who is Walt Disney? Who is Rosa Parks? Who is Princess Diana?

Walt Disney lived from 1901 to 1966. He's famous for all things Disney. He's an ENFP. He was charming. He got people to believe in him. He had big dreams. He imagined the happiest place on Earth. Then he made it happen. He created the first Disney theme park in 1955.

He was creative. He was independent. He was innovative. He led the way for **animated** movies. Animated refers to cartoons. In 1937, he created *Snow White and the Seven Dwarfs*. Making this movie cost a lot. As an ENFP, he focused on his dreams. He didn't focus on money. He almost lost a lot of money. But the film was a success.

You can get the MBTI codes for many Disney characters.
Who are your favorite Disney characters? Look them up!

Activists fight for change. Most activists are extroverts. They're known for being loud. Rosa Parks was an activist. But she was an introvert. She was an ISFJ. Parks lived from 1913 to 2005. She was an African American. On December 1, 1955, she made history. She refused to give up her seat to a white man. She made a statement. She broke the law on purpose. She was arrested. She helped start the civil rights movement. She helped fight for freedom for African Americans.

Parks had quiet strength. She was known for what she did, not what she said. She quietly resisted. She inspired people to fight for civil rights. She helped and protected her community.

Quiet people are not weak. The MBTI helps to show the many traits people can have. Can you think of other quiet heroes?

BIOGRAPHY

Dr. Merve Emre is Turkish-American. She has degrees from Harvard and Yale. She's a professor at Oxford University. She teaches English. In 2007, she worked for a marketing company. This is when she took the Myers-Briggs test. She's an ENTJ. Over 10 years later, she wrote a book about Myers-Briggs. Her book's title is *The Personality Brokers: The Strange History of Myers-Briggs and the Birth of Personality Testing*. Emre writes about the impacts of the test on society. She also writes about Isabel Myers and Katherine Briggs. She honors their work as inventors and mothers. She said, "A lot of the people who've read early versions of the book have been surprised to learn that Myers and Briggs were women in the first place ... they were highly educated and incredibly ambitious women." Emre lives in England. She has a husband and 2 children.

Princess Diana lived from 1961 to 1997. She was the Princess of Wales. She was an INFP. This makes sense. She cared deeply about people. She was very passionate about her causes. She visited hospitals. She visited homeless centers. She listened to people. She worked to ban land mines. She changed how people thought about diseases. She supported the arts. She worked hard for world peace. She was widely loved. She was called "the people's princess."

How do you help others? The MBTI shows there are different ways to serve.

WHO ARE YOU?
TAKE THE QUIZ!

What do you want to be when you grow up? Different types can be well-suited to the same job. Myers-Briggs is often used to match people to jobs.

- **Accountant, Police Officer, Librarian:** ISTJ
- **Banker, Nurse, Social Worker:** ISFJ
- **Social Worker, Journalist, Psychologist:** INFJ
- **Doctor, Judge, Scientist:** INTJ
- **Engineer, Computer Programmer, Pilot:** ISTP
- **Counselor, Graphic Designer, Physical Therapist:** ISFP
- **Artist, Chef, Naturalist:** INFP
- **Mathematician, Scientist, Software Developer:** INTP

- **Businessperson, Politician, Salesperson:** ESTP
- **Actor, Teacher, Musician:** ESFP
- **Musician, Politician, TV Reporter:** ENFP
- **Inventor, Lawyer, Writer:** ENTP
- **Judge, Military Officer, School Principal:** ESTJ
- **Doctor, Social Worker, Teacher:** ESFJ
- **Politician, Military Officer, Teacher:** ENFJ
- **Ceo, Salesperson, University Professor:** ENTJ

What is your spirit animal? These animals embody the spirit of the Myers-Briggs personality types.

- **Beaver:** ISTJ
- **Penguin:** ISFJ
- **Whale:** INFJ
- **Octopus:** INTJ
- **Cat:** ISTP
- **Sloth:** ISFP

- **Swan:** INFP
- **Owl:** INTP
- **Fox:** ESTP
- **Otter:** ESFP
- **Dolphin:** ENFP
- **Eagle:** ENTP

- **Queen Honeybee:** ESTJ
- **Elephant:** ESFJ
- **Dog:** ENFJ
- **Lion:** ENTJ

What type of student are you? Learning how to learn will help you be a better student.

- You plan your tasks. You turn your work in on time. You work best with structure: You're ESFJ, ISFJ, ESTJ, or ISTJ.

- You like open-ended tasks. You work best with a lot of freedom: You're ESFP, ISFP, ESTP, or ISTP.

- You like group projects. You work best when people care about you: You're INFJ, ENFJ, INFP, or ENFP.

- You research topics on your own. You won't quit until you mastered something. You work best when you can ask a lot of questions: You're INTJ, ENTJ, INTP, or ENTP.

What is your life motto? Myers-Briggs is based on how people see the world.

- Duty calls: ISTJ
- Love is all you need: ISFJ
- Change is good: INFJ
- We can do better: INTJ
- No problem is too big to be solved: ISTP
- You only live once: ISFP
- Beauty is life: INFP
- Data is king: INTP
- Do today. Don't wait for tomorrow: ESTP

- Live life to the fullest: ESFP
- The fun is in the journey: ENFP
- There are two sides of a coin: ENTP
- Law and order are above all else: ESTJ
- Get things done: ESFJ
- Teamwork makes the dream work: ENFJ
- Follow the leader: ENTJ

Glossary

activists (AK-tih-vists) people who fight for causes

advocate (AD-vuh-kit) champion or supporter

animated (AN-uh-may-tid) coming to life, cartoons

compatible (kuhm-PAT-uh-buhl) being able to get along with others

elaborate (ih-LAB-ur-it) complicated or hard

emotions (ih-MOH-shuhnz) feelings

idealists (eye-DEEL-ists) people who have big dreams and noble goals

indicator (IN-dih-kay-tur) tool that reveals something

introspective (in-truh-SPEK-tiv) reflective, self-aware

inventory (IN-vuhn-tor-ee) a type of test that is like a checklist

norms (NORMZ) standards used for comparing how far or close things are to a "normal" or typical response

observant (uhb-ZURV-uhnt) being aware and paying attention to details

psychiatrist (sye-KYE-uh-trist) medical doctor who studies how the mind works

psychology (sye-KAH-luh-jee) study of human behavior

rationalists (RASH-uh-nuhl-ists) thinkers

reliable (rih-LYE-uh-buhl) producing the same results consistently

self-report (SELF rih-PORT) to answer based on your own perceptions

valid (VAL-id) measuring what it intends to measure

Index